CAPTAIN WOODES ROGERS' VOYAGE ROUND THE WORLD 1708–1711

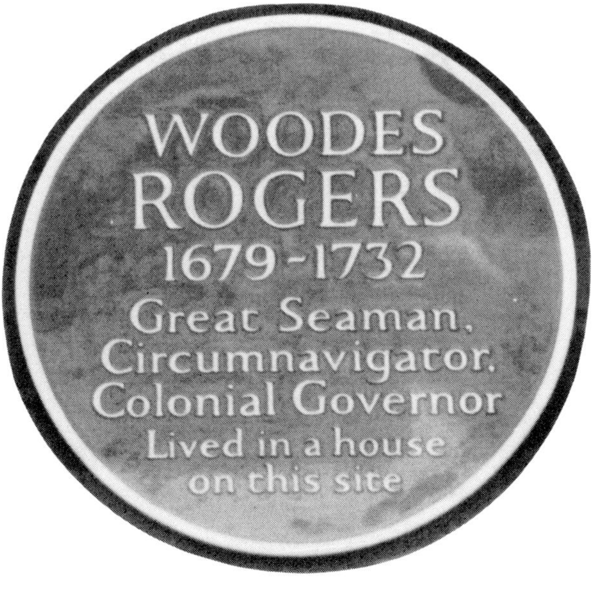

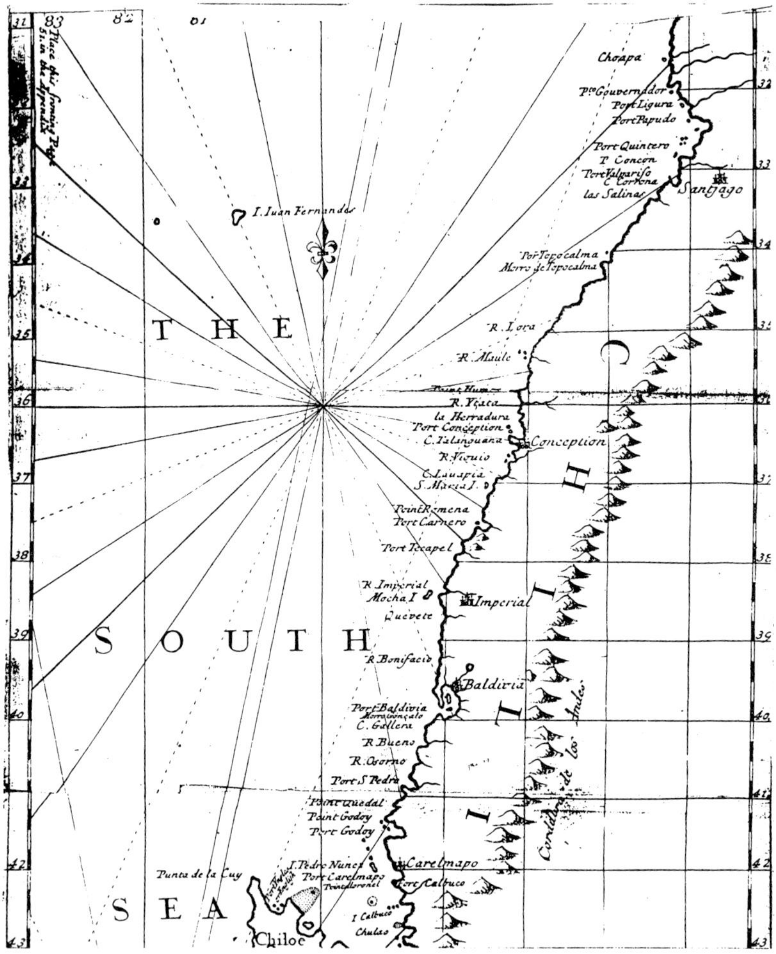

Map of The South Sea (Chile) showing Juan Fernandez, 1712, from Woodes Rogers' *A Cruising Voyage. . .* Drawn by R.S. Stephen. fronting p.51 in Appendix.

The Portuguese and Spanish voyages of discovery in the late fifteenth century to find new and direct routes to southern Asia hoped to obtain spices to make food more palatable. To reach the Pacific they had to circumnavigate a huge land mass that they initially believed to be Asia but which they came to accept was a New World. In 1493, the Spanish pope, Alexander VI, in a papal bull later ratified in the Treaty of Tordisillas, divided this New World between Spain and Portugal. The Treaty was never accepted by the other Atlantic states and infringements soon occurred, including those made by Bristol merchants such as Sir Thomas Wyndham and William Hawkins.

The Spaniard Hernan Cortés headed an expedition in 1518 to colonise the Mexican mainland and he began the complete subjugation of the Aztec empire. The gold mined by the Aztecs was systematically pillaged and transported, twice a year, in large, well-defended, treasure ships, from Acapulco in Mexico to Manilla in the Phillipines. From there they went to Spain. The richly laden Manilla–Acapulco treasure ships were seized on three occasions by English privateering expeditions led by Cavendish in 1587, Woodes Rogers in 1709 and Anson in 1743. Unsuccessful attempts were also made, such as that of Dampier in 1704.

Privateering voyages were given official approval through being issued with 'letters of marque, mart or reprisal' by the Admiralty Court. These licences authorised the possessors to take reprisals, either in war or peace, for losses sustained as a result of the action of foreigners. Proof of loss was required in the early seventeenth century and applicants were forbidden to recoup themselves in excess of their initial loss. In the late seventeenth century 'letters of marque' were given only in time of war, and for 'general reprisals' against the enemy. Privateers did not carry a cargo and were fitted out and armed by merchants as private men-of-war to cruise against the enemy and to seize prizes. From 1702–1713 there occurred the War of Spanish Succession and 'letters of marque' declarations were given to 127 Bristol ships, among which were the *Duke* and *Dutchess*.

Such privateering expeditions had to take care not to infringe the monopoly rights of English joint stock companies such as the East India Company which had come into existence in the reign of Elizabeth in 1600. At the beginning of the eighteenth century this company traded in India through a number of fortified factories at Madras, Bombay, Calcutta and Surat. From these bases the company organised English trade with the spice islands of the East Indies. As they sailed through the Malacca Straits into the Indian Ocean the *Duke* and *Dutchess* obtained much needed supplies at Batavia and Bantam. Unfortunately Woodes Rogers engaged in some speculations there and it was these which particularly aroused the suspicions of the governors of the East India Company.

To Captain Woodes Rogers belongs the rare distinction, at that time, shared with other Englishmen such as Francis Drake and Thomas Cavendish, of circumnavigating the world. Unlike William Dampier he had managed to hold the motley crews of privateers together, achieved coordinated efforts like the sack of Guayaquil and the capture of the annual Spanish treasure ship, and brought most of his men back to the Thames in 1711 unharmed. For his times Woodes Rogers was a man of some sensitivity who allowed Mass on board ship for his Spanish prisoners, who kept a public, written, log of all decisions, open for amendment, and secured the agreement of his crews for the sharing of plunder. Throughout the voyage he abided by the decisions of most of the Councils held on board one or other of the ships.

Woodes Rogers had not intended to circumnavigate the globe when he set out on 1 August 1708, and when he returned to the Dutch river Tetzel on 23 July 1711 he faced the hostility of the governors of the East India Company. The governors were determined to protect their monopoly of trade with India and Cathay, which they had secured in 1600, and to debar all interlopers from the outports like Bristol from Eastern commerce. The capture of a Spanish treasure ship, and nineteen other prizes, was not seen as a licence for supposed trading with the East Indies. This highly successful privateering voyage was followed by a three year battle in the Courts during the course of which Woodes Rogers became bankrupt and the crews of the *Duke* and *Dutchess* remained virtually unpaid. The crews twice petitioned the House of Lords, in June 1714 and August 1715, claiming they were "perishing from Want of Bread, and daily thrown into Gaols, or in danger of being so."

Although he had a house in Queen Square, Bristol, and was married to the daughter of Admiral Sir William Whetstone, Woodes Rogers was not wealthy, and there are grounds for believing he had sustained personal losses while trading with Newfoundland. So far as is known, his wife had no source of income while he was at sea, and was forced to leave Queen Square and move, with her three children, to her father's house in St. Michael's Park. While at Batavia, Rogers unwisely speculated in arrack, a spirit distilled from coco-sap or rice, which proved a bad investment, and was mentioned during the Chancery proceedings of Creagh v Rogers. He needed to make a lot of money and was eager to engage in privateering in 1708. In this he was not alone.

When Captain William Dampier was engaged as pilot to the voyage he was in a state of great poverty and money had to be advanced to enable him to equip himself. In 1698 Dampier had been sent by the Admiralty as commander of the *Roebuck* to explore southern New Guinea and New Holland. The ship was unseaworthy and sank on the return voyage as a result of which Dampier had to face 3 trials by courts martial, and lost 3 years' pay. Dampier had written at least three important navigational works before the *Duke* and *Dutchess*' voyage. *A New Voyage Round the World*, published in 1697, contained the first description of a typhoon, and was based on travels made in the years 1679–91 in various ships, amounting to a circumnavigation. In 1699 came his *Discourse of the Trade Winds, Breezes, Storms, Seasons of the Year, Tides and Currents of the Torrid Zone throughout the World*, which proved of great assistance to other navigators. His book *A Voyage to New Holland . . . in the year 1699*, appeared in 1703. He had been the commodore of the voyage to the South Seas in 1703–1706 and had returned without either of the two ships with which he had set out – the *Cinque Ports*, galley, and the *St. George*.

As a result of his conduct of that voyage the owners were planning to sue him for the loss of the ships. The daughter of Thomas Estcourt, one of the owners, (Elizabeth Cresswell, nee Estcourt), married the wealthy Wiltshire landowner Richard

Cresswell who was determined to get Dampier to Court. Dampier however was fortunate enough to persuade Bristol merchants to back another South Seas voyage and he set out from England before Cresswell could prepare the case. Captain Dampier therefore had very strong motives for departing on a privateering voyage and he knew the South Seas better than any other Englishman.

Captain Edward Cooke had lost two ships within 8 months prior to agreeing to serve as second captain of the *Dutchess*. He was part-owner in both cases of ship and cargo. The *Mead*, galley, 20 guns, had been set upon by four Dunkirk privateers in the Channel. He lost all his masts except the mainmast, the ship was on fire and badly holed, and he and several of his men were badly wounded. He was subsequently made captain of a newly built galley of 20 guns and sailed for Leghorn, but near Oran was attacked by a 50 gun French man-of-war. They fought from midday till evening when another French man-of-war arrived and he surrendered. Captain Cooke also needed to repair his fortunes in a hurry.

The Bristol merchants who listened to Dampier and raised the money for the *Duke* and *Dutchess*' voyage issued 256 shares of £103 10s. each. They were quite clear in their *Orders and Instructions* to Captain Woodes Rogers, dated 14 July 1708. The enterprise was intended to seize the Spanish treasure ships.

> . . . But our grand design Being to seek out one or bothe the Ships belonging to Acapulco in South America . . . If you are so fortunate to come up with her you are to attack and use all possible means to take her, which we doubt not of through your Bravery, especially promoted by the vast Treasure you may expect to share for your reward.
>
> Yet notwithstanding if you should, in your passage into the South Seas, or on the Coast of Peru or Chili, meet with and take purchase so considerable that you think it will be worth your while, Then return with such Booty directly for England, or touch att any place for the better securing what you have, as your Councill will direct and judge fit . . .[1]

The owners commissioned a ". . . new-built Shipp called *Duke*, burthened about 350 tonns and of 6 and 30 guns, now lying at the Key in this City."[2] They paid Thomas Clements £1,310 for the new hull, and another £6,888 on cordage, guns, canvas, masts and sails, to various Bristol and London companies.[3] The *Dutchess* too was purchased as a new hull and cost £850: ". . . the new-built Shipp called *Duchesse*".[4] The additional 'Outsetts' on masts, anchors, guns, canvas, rope and cordage, amounted to £4,140 12s. The *Dutchess* weighed about 260 tonns and had 26 guns. In February 1707 the owners sent Mr. J. Welch to London to enquire in the shipyards for guns from captured prizes, or good English guns. He was to return with 42 guns throwing about 15 lbs, not exceeding 16 lbs wt., 4 guns throwing about 24 lbs wt each, 8 guns about 5 lbs to 6 lbs wt., 12 guns about 2 lbs, and 4 carronades for the topps.[5] The Bristolians who invested in the enterprise included some of the city's leading citizens. They included John Hollidge with 10 shares, (Mayor 1708), Christopher Shuter with 30 shares, (Mayor 1711), John Romsey with 15 shares, (Town Clerk), Sir John Hawkins with 10 shares, (Mayor 1701), Thomas Clements with 4 shares, (Sheriff 1709), Philip Freake with 22 shares, (Sheriff, 1708), and John Batchelor with 16 shares, (Alderman and wealthy merchant). Dr. Thomas Dover, a famous Bristol physician of Magdalen Hall, Oxford, and Gonville and Caius, Cambridge invested in 32 shares, and, at the age of 46 and totally unaccustomed to a seafaring life, became second captain of the *Duke*, Captain of marines, and President of the Council on board with 2 votes. Thomas Goldney II, a Quaker grocer, in 1703 had inherited a considerable fortune from his father-in-law Thomas Speed, and invested in 36 shares.

For these shrewd and distinguished citizens to have invested so heavily in this privateering venture the case must have been exceptionally convincing. The two ships were newly built for the enterprise. They chose as pilot William Dampier because of his exceptional knowledge of the South Seas, and were of course unaware of Alexander Selkirk's and William Sheltram's subsequent testimony regarding the previous loss of the *Cinque Ports*, galley, and the *St. George*.

> . . . Dampier, having been several voyages to the South Seas before this Voyage, . . . must needs know that the worms there doe eat ships extreamly hard, and as bad as in any other part of the world . . . the *not* sheathing of the ships *St. George* and *Cinque Ports* galley was the loss of both those ships for they perished by being worm eaten . . .[6]

I have found no evidence of sheathing of either the *Duke* or the *Dutchess*, and while it is true that many East Indiamen were sheathed, the bulk of Bristol privateers and merchantmen sailed without sheathing.

For Bristol merchants the opening up of new trading opportunities might be thought to have carried weight, and while Woodes Rogers in his introduction to his *Voyage* is most persuasive about the importance of opening up trade to the river Plate, yet at ground level the officers and men were quite clear what they were about.

> That we went out as Private Men of War and *not* as trading ships, And that no sort of Merchandise was shipped on board said Ships to trade withall, . . ., we drove no trade or made any purchase att Bouton or Batavia or any other part of East Indies more than for Necessarys and Provisions.[7]

They looked to obtain the prize money and a share of treasure since this was a privateering voyage.

According to Capt. Edward Cooke in 1712, Dampier had tried to take the Manilla–Acapulco treasure ship in 1704 but had found it too powerfully armed and had been forced to withdraw, but

> Captain Dampier never gave over the Project, till he had prevail'd with some able Persons at Bristol to venture upon an Undertaking, which might turn to a prodigious Advantage.[8]

Cooke asserted "Peru and Chile afford inexhaustible Streams of Gold and Silver, the main Objects of Worldly Men's Desires." The *Duke* and *Dutchess* were therefore larger ships with a heavier armament than Dampier's former undertaking had enjoyed.

The owners also learnt from the mutinies and difficulties that had beset Dampier's voyage of 1703, particularly after the death of Captain Pickering. They did not have Selkirk's or Sheltram's evidence of 1712 that Dampier, Stradling and Morgan "managed all things in hugger-mugger among themselves and without the knowledge of the ship's Company . . ."[9] and that Dampier failed in

> not calling Councills of his Officers as he ought to have done, or if he did call them, in refusing to be ruled by them or to follow their advices, but . . . deciding all things in such manner as himself pleased, contrary to their advice to the very great Damage of the Owners of the said Ship and to the loss of the whole voyage . . .[10]

Nevertheless, the owners of the *Duke* and *Dutchess* acted as if they had heard something of these problems in 1708. They appointed a

Council for the voyage with Thomas Dover as President, and drew up a detailed Constitution. Rogers says that

> in pursuance of this, we held frequent councils to make such agreements as occasion required, that the officers who signed them might see them put into execution; for without this method we could never have performed the voyage, nor kept together . . .[11]

He also had

> a daily account kept in a public book of all our transactions, which lay open to everyone's view, and where any thing was reasonably objected against, it was corrected.[12]

On June 15 1708 the two new ships, *Duke* and *Dutchess*, were towed down the Avon by rowing boats from Hung Road out to Kingroad and stayed there until August 1, waiting for the convoy to Cork to assemble. The crews that the officers had managed to assemble consisted of many "ordinary Fellows, and not fit for our Employment".[13] They managed to replace some of them at Cork as some ran away, and "oui Crew were constantly marrying whilst we stayed at Cork, tho' they expected to sail immediately."[14] The ships sailed for Tenerife on September 1 with a complement of

> 333, of which above one Third were Foreigners from most Nations; several of her Majesty's Subjects on board were Tinkers, Taylors, Hay-Makers, Pedlers, Fidlers etc, one Negro, and about ten Boys. With this mix'd Gang we hop'd to be well mann'd . . .[15]

On the 11 September they stopped and searched a Swedish frigate of 270 tons and 22 guns but, after a cursory examination, could not find any contraband on board, and Woodes Rogers, anxious to make progress, therefore allowed her to go. This provoked a mutiny by part of the crew who wanted time to "rummage" further. He put 10 of his men in irons, including the Boatswain, Giles Cash. Three days after this half the crew mutinied again to secure the release of the Boatswain. Woodes Rogers got the ringleader to come to speak with him on the Quarter Deck where the officers seized him. One of the man's comrades was then forced to give the ringleader a public flogging. Woodes Rogers wrote,

Governor Rogers and Family from Samuel Ireland, *Graphic Illustrations of Hogarth* Vol 2, 1799.

> This Mutiny would not have been easily lay'd were it not for the number of our Officers, which we begin to find very necessary to bring our Crew to Order and Discipline, which is always very difficult in Privateers, and without which 'tis impossible to carry on any distant Undertaking like ours.[16]

The ships crossed the Tropic of Cancer on 24 September having anchored for two days at Orotava on Tenerife. They reached St. Vicent in the Cape Verde Islands on 30 September and set about replenishing their water supply.

> Oct. 1. We cleared our Ship yesterday, but it blow'd too hard to row our Boat-Loads of empty Butts ashoar, and we could do but little to Wooding and Watering, till this morning we were forc'd to get a Rope from the Ship to the watering-place, which is a good half-mile from our anchoring place, and so haul'd our empty Casks ashore by Boat-loads, in order to have 'em burnt and clean'd in the Inside, being Oil-Casks, and for want of cleaning our Water stunk insufferably. I borrowed a Cooper from the *Dutchess*, and having five of my own, made quick dispatch.[17]

The *Duke* and *Dutchess* sailed for Brazil on 8 October, arrived at the Falkland Islands on 30 November, and encountered very bad weather as they rounded the Horn on 11 January 1709. In trying to lower the *Dutchess*' mainyard, as a violent gale approached on 5 January, the sail went into the sea and dragged the boat round so that she took in a great deal of water.

> The Sea had broke in the Cabin-windows, and over their Stern, filling their steerage and Waste, and had like to have spoil'd several men, but God be thank'd all was otherwise indifferent well with 'em, only they were intolerably cold, and everything wet.[18]

On 10 January they reached the furthest South that anyone had yet been, Lat. 61.53 and Long. W of London 79.58. By 1 February they were sailing up the coast of Chile and anchored and watered at Juan Fernandez. Here they found the mariner Alexander Selkirk. In the Public Record Office Chancery Lane is a five page testament of the Scotsman, written on 18 July 1712, and entered in the case of Cresswell v Dampier. The document was recently discovered by C.D. Lee.[19] Selkirk's deposition was made one month after the appearance in print of Capt. Edward Cooke's *A Voyage to the South Sea*. The book contained the first published account of Selkirk's experiences on Juan Fenandez and these are believed to have given rise to the story of Robinson Crusoe.

C.D. Lee argues that Selkirk was the foremastman of the *Cinque Ports* galley, not the Sail Master as he claimed, and that he had played a leading part in the mutiny against Captain Stradling in February 1704. I do not find this view convincing. Woodes Rogers in 1708 accepted that Selkirk had been Master, and Captain William Dampier confirmed it and recommended him. Rogers wrote,

> He had been on the Island four Years and four Months, being left there by Capt. Stradling in the *Cinque Ports*: his Name was Alexander Selkirk, a Scotchman, who had been Master of the *Cinque Ports*, a ship that came here last with Captain Dampier, who told me that this was the best Man in her, so I immediately agreed with him to be a Mate on board our Ship.[20]

Selkirk said he had asked to stay on Juan Fernandez because he knew the *Cinque Ports* was full of holes and unseaworthy: that the *Cinque Ports* subsequently foundered suggests that he had been right. He knew ships put into Juan Fernandez to refit and obtain water but never anticipated waiting four years. Before the *Cinque Ports* sailed from Juan Fernandez Selkirk changed his mind again but was not allowed back on board. Having served for a year as Mate on the *Duke*, Selkirk was promoted to be the Sail Master of the *Batchelor*, under Capt. Thomas Dover, and sailed the treasure ship back to the Tetzel and then to London. The renamed *Batchelor* had formerly been the *Nuestra Senora de la Incarnacion Disenganio*, of 450 tons.

The *Duke* and *Dutchess* began their first privateering cruise in February 1709. They captured the *Assumption* on the 15th and then the *Santa Josepha*. On April 2 they captured the *Ascension*, 400 tons, with 50–60 negroes on board, and the same evening they captured the *Joseph*. On the 15th they seized the 260 tons *Havre de Grace* which they then fitted out as a privateer and renamed *Marquis*, under the command of Capt. Edward Cooke. However, it proved an unsuitable ship and was subsequently sold at Batavia in June 1710.[21]

> Att a Committee held on board the *Dutchesse* at sea, off the island Gorgona, [their base for the next 2 months] August 8th. 1709
> Memorandum: The *Marquis*, not answering our expectations but proves Crank and sails heavy, we now advise Capt. Cooke to heave

the *Dutchess*' 2 old heavy guns overboard and 20 boxes of snuff, with 2 spare topmasts, and bring his ship more by the stern, stowing everything as low as possible in the ship to indevor to make her swifter, and if he finds any more necessary for the benefit of the ship, we desire him to do it.[22]

The ships' Council had taken the decision on 12 April to attack the town of Guayaquil, (population 100,000) and at midnight on 21 April the crew could see the lights of Guayaquil burning. On the 22nd they captured four barques trying to escape down the river and on St. George's day, the 23rd, they stormed the town. A large ransom of 25,500 pieces of eight was negotiated if they did not set the town on fire. The female population was apparently treated with some respect:

Some of the largest Gold Chains were conceal'd and wound about their Middles, Legs and Thighs etc. but the Gentlewomen in these hot Countries, being very thin clad with Silk and fine Linnen . . . our Men, by pressing, felt the Chains etc. with their Hands on the Outside of the Ladys' Apparel, and, by their Linguist, modestly desired the Gentlewomen to take 'em off and surrender 'em.[23]

At least this is what Woodes Rogers says happened although he was well aware how difficult it was to control the privateers at any time.

The problems of the division of the spoils and of what constituted plunder constantly exercised the minds of the privateers. On 29 June a Committee, including representatives of the crews, regulated the award of plunder taken at Guayaquil. In addition the wounded were awarded "smart money", and the boat crews that attacked the *Havre de Grace* received 4 bales of goods over and above their shares. A good suit of clothes was given to each man that took part in the expedition up the river. The *Agreements* regarding plunder that had been signed in Bristol with the owners proved difficult to apply in practice.

For we found it would be next to a miracle to keep the Men in both Ships under Command and willing to fight resolutely on occasion, if we held 'em to the Letter of Agreement with the Owners, which was not duly considered of at home.[24]

Again on October 8th, at a Committee on board the *Dutchess*, an agreement was made between the officers and men consisting of 7 regulations about plunder. Among these it was agreed that

(2) That what is 'Plunder' shall be adjudg'd by the Superior Officers and Agents in each Ship.
(3) . . . when any Prize is taken by Storm in Boarding, then whatsoever is taken shall be his own as followeth: A Sailor or Landsman £10; Any Officer below the Carpenter £20; A Mate, Gunner, Boatswain and Carpenter £40; A Lieutenant or Master £80; And the Captains £100 over and above the Gratuity promised by the Owners . . .[25]

Several more ships were captured as the ships cruised four times round their base at Gorgona. There were now four privateers since the renamed *Havre de Grace* (*Marquis*) and the *Joseph* had been crewed from the *Duke* and *Dutchess*. They visited the Galapagos and laid in a stock of turtles and then sailed to the Tres Marias Islands. By the 13 December they still had not seen the two Manilla–Acapulco Spanish treasure ships for which they had come this far, and which were now a month overdue.

Eventually at daybreak on 22 December the *Nuestra Senora de la Incarnacion Disenganio*, 450 tons, with 193 men on board, was sighted. The action lasted one and half hours before the treasure ship surrendered and was escorted into Porto Seguro, eventually to be renamed the *Batchelor*. A keen lookout was kept for the consort of the treasure ship and it was sighted on Christmas Day. The *Dutchess* and *Marquis* immediately engaged the *Bigonia* but were outfought by the 900 tons treasure ship with a crew of 450 and passengers in addition. It was armed with 40 guns and 40 swivels and put up a vigorous fight. The *Duke* arrived on the 27 December and the three ships renewed the action. After two hours the *Duke*'s mainmast was disabled and from one of their tops on the *Bigonia* a fireball fell on the *Duke*'s quarterdeck which blew up some gunpowder in the steerage and badly injured the owners' agent, Carlton Vanbrugh. The *Dutchess* had to make for the shore to repair her rigging while the *Marquis* and the *Duke* continued the action. The fight ended when the Duke received a second shot in the mainmast which shattered much of her rigging. The actual fighting lasted about seven hours. 20 had been killed or wounded on the *Dutchess*: 11 had been wounded on the *Duke*, and two had been burnt on the *Marquis* before the ships were called off.

On 1 January 1710 from Porto Seguro in Brazil the prisoners were sent off to Acapulco. After a refit at Porto Seguro the *Duke*, *Dutchess*, the renamed *Batchelor* and the *Marquis* sailed for Guam and arrived on 11 March. They left for Batavia on 21 March and arrived there a month later where the *Marquis* was sold. After a long stay the three ships set sail again on 23 October from Java Head to cross the Indian Ocean for the Cape of Good Hope which they reached on 28 December. Carlton Vanbrugh died here as did several seamen, and he was buried in a churchyard, with salutes from the ships' guns, on 12 February, 1711. The *Duke*, *Dutchess* and *Batchelor* sailed from the Cape on the 6 April in a convoy with 16 Dutch ships, including several men-of-war, and six East India Company ships. The fleet arrived in the Tetzel, Holland, on 23 July 1711 at about 2 pm where they waited for the flood tide to carry them to a safe anchorage in 6 fathoms, 2 miles off shore.[26]

Seamen who had joined the *Duke*, *Dutchess* and *Batchelor* at Batavia or at the Cape were discharged on 1 August. For better security, between the 4th and 6th August the ships were moved to an anchorage called the Vlicler, while the East India Company's boats left for England,

> it being by a particular Order from the Owners . . . we being oblig'd to wait there, fearing the India company would be troublesome, altho' we had dealt for nothing but Necessaries in India.[27]

James Hollidge, one of the owners, got the officers and crews to swear affidavits before a Notary Publick on 10th August "in Answer to what the East India Company had alleged against us."[28] On the 31st James Hollidge came aboard the *Duke* and *Dutchess* and took an inventory of the plate, gold and pearls that were in the ships. Nothing was to be taken ashore from the boats lest it should prejudice the insurance. Before leaving he also took a list of the seamen to get protection for them from the Press Gang which would be waiting for them as soon as they reached the Thames.[29]

The three ships joined a waiting convoy of men-of-war at anchor in the Tetzel on the 20th September. They sailed for England at 10 am on the 22nd but in the afternoon the *Batchelor* had to be taken in tow and the ships returned to the Tetzel where the convoy agreed to wait for them. Eventually the ships weighed anchor and set sail again, arriving at the Downs on the 1st October. The 3 boats finally arrived at Erith, near Woolwich, on the Thames on 14 October after a remarkable voyage. They had captured 20 ships and sailed home with one of the two annual treasure ships. In addition, aboard the *Duke*, were 3 large chests containing plate, money, jewels and gold dust. Aboard the *Dutchess* were four chests of pearls, plate, gold and precious stones. Above all they had brought back their ships, most of the crews, and a large collection of maps, considered by Edward Cooke to be invaluable in improving the knowledge of those coasts and seas:

> by bringing home the Spanish manuscript coasting maps taken from their ships, being the only accounts to be relied on by such as shall hereafter sail into those parts, all our adventures having barely touched at some places and never so much as seen the most; whereas these are descriptions approved by the constant practice of about 200 years that nation has been trading to all the ports along that coast.[30]

It is probably true to say that these maps contributed to the formation of the South Sea Company in 1711.

The condition of the boats gave some cause for concern. The *Dutchess* had sustained damage in rounding the Magellan Straits and in the course of their sea fights in the South Seas the *Duke* and *Dutchess* had received numerous hits. Despite being newly-built the *Duke* had leaked quite badly before any of this happened.

> Whereas Woodes Rogers, Commander of the *Duke*, Friggott, has had a leaky Ship ever since we left California, and having an opportunity to stop and land att Batavia, but want of good Judgement and not heaving her keel out, the Leake still continued the same, Capt. Courtney admonished him to careen the ship *Duke* againe whilst att the Island of Horne when all things were ready, and before he took in his Goods and Guns, but he would not, alledging that his Leake was nothing . . .[31]

The other Captains and officers had come to distrust Rogers and suspected he intended to leave the other ships and to deal in contraband goods on his own account;

> Having good Reasons to believe the said Woodes Rogers designes to goe to Brazill, Newfoundland, or att least to leave us att Sea, being well assured he makes this a Pretext to cover his Insideous Designs, we therefore, on Behalf of the Owners and selves Protest against the said Woodes Rogers for such his Neglect and against all Contraband goods, that may endamage our Owners or selves, Ship or Company . . .[32]

The 'Pretext' referred to was Woodes Rogers' proposal to the Council that he might "have leave to take his ship to Sardinia Bay". The return voyage across the Pacific and by way of the Cape of Good Hope was necessary because of the bad condition of the ships. They could not have withstood the gales around the Horn a second time.

Inevitably, in the course of the long and arduous voyage, there had been disputes in Council. Captain Edward Cooke recorded some of them. When the *Nuestra Senora de la Incarnacion Disenganio* had been captured there were "hot Disputes about appointing a Commander for the Manila Ship, being a Prize of considerable Value."[33] Thomas Dover owned shares in the enterprise and was President of Council, and he believed he should command the ship. Woodes Rogers and several others of the officers wanted Edward Cooke, second Captain to Stephen Courtney on the *Dutchess*, to command her, or Captain Frye, formerly second Lieutenant on the *Duke*. Edward Cooke voted against it and proposed with Stephen Courtney and several others that Thomas Dover should command, with Captain Frye and Captain Stretton as second Captains. Against this Woodes Rogers argued that Thomas Dover's violent temper would endanger the valuable prize,

> that capable Men cannot act well under him, and himself is incapable . . . Confusion follows a mix'd Command, which would be very pernicious in this Case, which it highly concerns us to be careful of . . . This is my Opinion. January 9 1709/10 Woodes Rogers.[34]

Woodes Rogers lost the vote and Captain Thomas Dover became the Commander of the *Batchelor* with Frye and Stretton as second Captains and with Alexander Selkirk as Master.

Much more serious however was the Committee Minute of 19 June 1711 at a Council held on the *Batchelor* while sailing from the Cape up to the Tetzel. John Parker's Committee Book records the officers, including Captains Courtney, Cooke, Dover, and Dampier as deeply contemptuous of Woodes Rogers'

> being a man whose Circumstances are very indifferent for whatever Reasons, . . . (the Committee) have considered since Mr. Vanbrugh is dead, and had part of the charge of the aforesaid Gold, etc . . . We have herein asserted we do hold itt highly Necessary to remove the aforesaid Commoditys.

The cause of this gratuitous insult was ostensibly:

> that the *Duke*, Frigatt, has been a long time Leaky till now of late, and We being informed by the Coxwain and others of their men, that

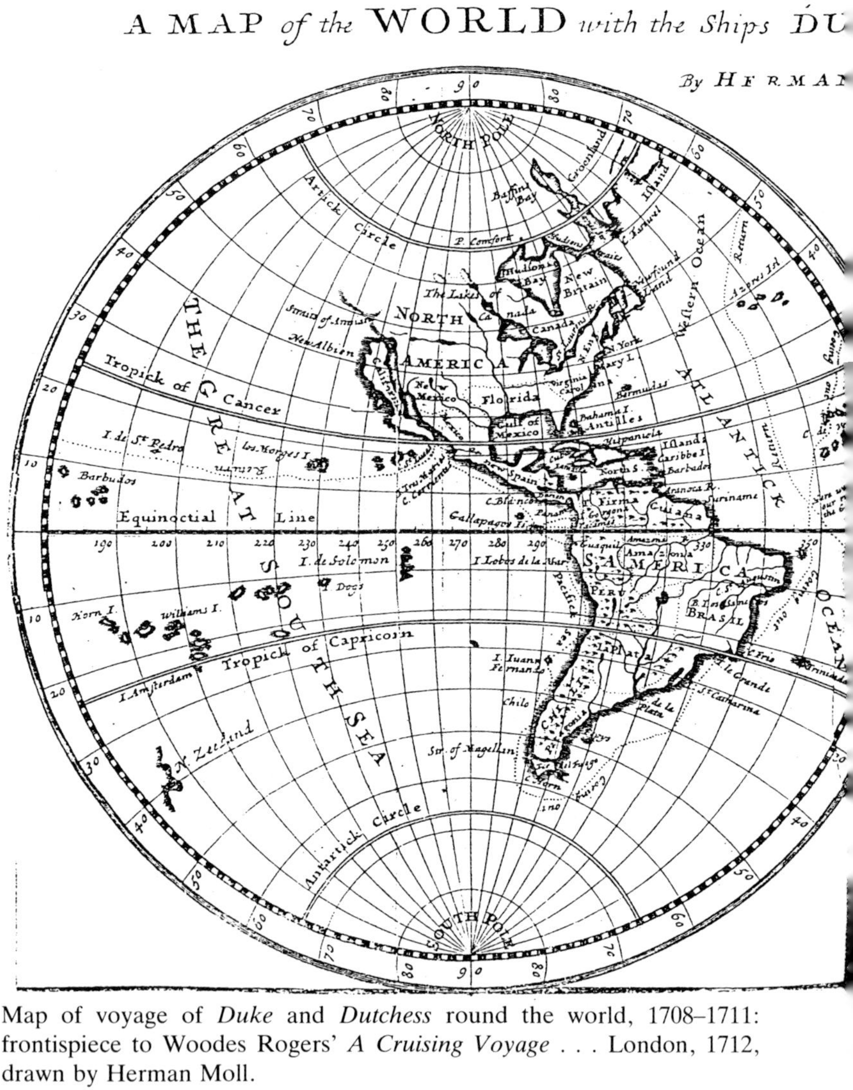

Map of voyage of *Duke* and *Dutchess* round the world, 1708–1711: frontispiece to Woodes Rogers' *A Cruising Voyage* . . . London, 1712, drawn by Herman Moll.

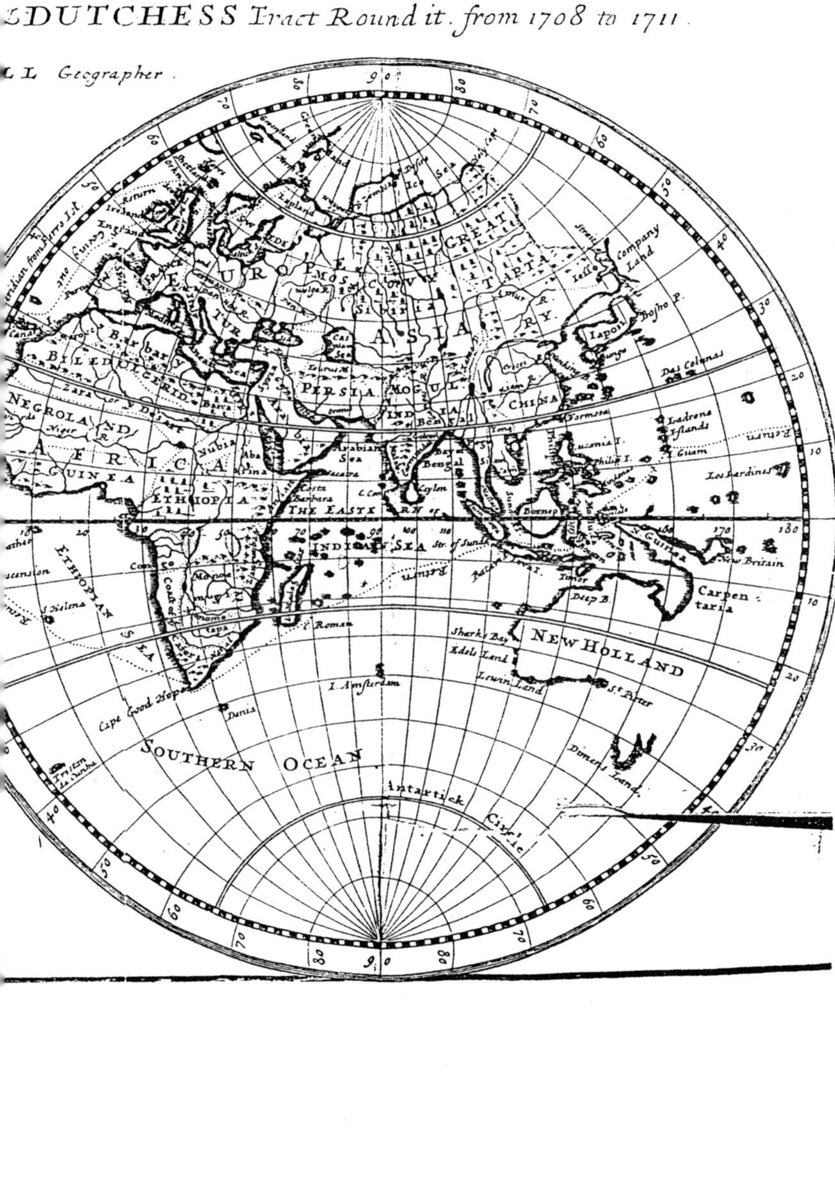
DUTCHESS Tract Round it. from 1708 to 1711.
Geographer
EUROPE
ASIA
AFRICA
MOSCOVY
GREAT TARTARY
PERSIA
INDIA
CHINA
Siberia
Barbary
BILEDULGERID
NEGROLAND
GUINEA
ETHIOPIA
Nubia
Arabian Sea
Bay of Bengal
Ceylon
Borneo
Iapon
Formosa
Ladrone Islands
Guam
Philip I.
Company Land
Das Colunas
Los Jardines
THE EASTERN OCEAN
INDIAN SEA
Str. of Sunda
Timor
Deep B.
New Britain
Carpentaria
NEW HOLLAND
Sharks Bay
Edels Land
Lewins Land
St. Peter
I. Amsterdam
Cape Good Hope
Dimens Land
SOUTHERN OCEAN
Antartick Circle
St. Helena
Caspian Sea
Ice Sea
Ireland
England
France
Lapland
New Guinea

last time they towed the *Batchelor* (wch was a small Gale and smooth Water), that then she made twice the Water as she did before; And now we are gotten well to the North where We may Expect strong Gales and great Seas; Itt's our Opinion for the Interest of the Owners and Selves to remove all Gold, Plate, Pearls, Jewells and Ear Rings out of the *Duke* and to put it on board the *Dutchess*, she being a tite ship, and where we suspect less Danger.[35]

Woodes Rogers ignored the resolutions of the Council and no treasure was transferred at sea. Relations on board between him and his fellow officers must have been icy at times, but nevertheless, he brought the ships home together with their prize, loaded with treasure, and having circumnavigated the globe.

When the *Duke*, *Dutchess* and *Batchelor* arrived at the Tetzel on 23 July 1711, together with the 6 E. India Company's ships, agents of that company in Amsterdam immediately sent a letter to London informing the Governors of the East India Company of their arrival.[36] Warned by George and Isaac Clifford in Amsterdam the Governors resolved to seize the *Duke* and *Dutchess*, together with their Spanish prize, whenever they could get their hands on them and appointed Francis White, John Spencer and Daniel Hilman, with as many persons as they needed to do the job.[37] The Attorney General had received a petition from the owners, who had somehow learnt of the intentions of the Company, and he had already made some proposals to the Company which they had rejected.[38]

Meanwhile, Alderman Batchelor, John Romsey, and Thomas Palmer travelled from Bristol and met the Governors of the Company on 17 August to protest their innocence. No trade had been carried on by the vessels. If the Company persisted in carrying out their threat to seize the ships the result would be fatal to the owners and a great loss of revenue to H.M. Customs as the owners would have to sell their plunder abroad. There was no meeting of minds. The Court of Governors said "they have reason to differ in Opinion . . .", and were going ahead with their original intentions. The owners approached the Governors again on 12 September and Mr. Sheriff Eyles was approved as a Mediator, "to find out an Expedient for reconciling the Differences between them (the Owners) and the Company".[39] The owners therefore decided to bring the three ships to England. Woodes Rogers sailed up the Thames to Erith and anchored on 14 October.

The men hired by the East India Company then made an effort

to seize the anchored Spanish prize but were beaten off by the crew aboard.[40] Subsequently the *Batchelor* was seized, and the news was reported to the Governors on 17 October.[41] The record of the seizure was then entered in the Exchequer Court, and this persuaded the Bristol owners, John Romsey, Thomas Palmer and Mr. Cowles to make another effort at an accommodation.[42] The three met three Governors on a number of occasions and finally agreed on a sum (£6,000) which would satisfy the Governors.[43] John Sawley was paid £107 10s. "for seizing the Ship *Batchellour*", but I have no record of any attempt to seize the treasure on the *Duke* or *Dutchess*.[44] A bribe of £161 5s. was made to some unnamed person and the engrossed Covenant was signed on 18 March.

Back at Wapping the press gangs had been at work. The *Duke* and *Dutchess* were Letter of Marque ships, their Captains having obtained their Commissions from the Lord High Admiral, Prince George of Denmark. This had taken the form of a warrant directed to the Judge of the Admiralty Court. Woodes Rogers and Stephen Courtney would have attended the Court and made a declaration as to the ships' tunnage, guns, munitions, number of crew and names of officers. They were then legally allowed to attack enemy ships and to secure prizes. Their crews were normally paid and also had prize money, but they could claim no exemption from the press gangs. As soon as a privateer or merchantman docked, rowing boats from H.M. ships came alongside and sought to press the fittest of the crew, using force if need be. Sometimes captains hid their best men in the hold for fear of losing them to serve on the Men-of-War. James Hollidge had taken a list of the men aboard the *Duke* and *Dutchess* on 31 August to get them protection from impressment, but apparently his efforts were unsuccessful. Stephen Creagh had to pay Counsel's fees and 'fees of protection', and other charges, "in getting clear most of the men when Impressed at Wapping".[45]

When the ships had been anchored in the Tetzel, and before the voyage to the Thames, various agents touting for legal business offered to look after the interests of the crews. Stephen Creagh, who had been part-owner of two privateers, managed to induce 209 of the crews to sign a paper appointing him their agent in return for 5% of their eventual receipts. Woodes Rogers employed two other agents, Ward and Campbell, to look after his interests. On 11 January 1711/12, Creagh got the complaint brought before the Court of Chancery, citing the owners and the

Captains as guilty of irregular practices, and charging Woodes Rogers with "fraud against the Owners".

The warehousing of the prize goods began on 11 December and Robert Patterson was put in charge.[46] He claimed £311 10s. for 623 days at 10s. a day, and it would appear that by August 1713 the last goods had been disposed of. The transfer of the goods to the warehouse was carefully monitored by Stephen Creagh, as agent for the officers and men, and by the agents Ward and Campbell for Woodes Rogers and the owners. There was a mutual understanding between the agents over the custody of the keys. The sales began on February 11, 1711/12, and from 27 February at the Marine Coffee House, Birchin Lane in Cornhill, London, where the allotments of goods were "sold by the candle".[47] There were 9 public sales from 27 February 1712 to May 1713 and the total sum received from the sales amounted to £147,975 12s. 4½d., of which £22,387 2s. 5d. came from private contract sales. The Spanish prize ship *Batchelor* was sold for £895 0s.[48]

The Chancery Proceeding, Creagh v Rogers, dated 11 January 1712 came before Rt. Hon. Simon Harcourt, the Lord Chancellor, and his decision was given on 12 December 1712. The profits of the sales were to be divided into thirds, two of which were to go to the owners and one to the crew. No agency money was to be deducted from any officer or member of the crews other than from those 209 who signed the papers. The costs were to be paid out before any distribution of money occurred. In every case relating to the allocation of costs the Lord Chancellor decided against the owners. The Customs payments had totalled £27,524 15s.[49]

If the total profits of the sales had been divided as the Court had decreed, the owners would have received £98,650 and the crews £49,325. However, after paying expenses the owners received only £50,109 8s. 10d. Among the larger items charged to them were –

East India Co.	6,161	5s.	0d.
Wages in lieu of shares	12,262	1s.	5d.
Provisions in Holland	8,720	8s.	1d.
Outsetts on *Duke* and *Dutchess*	13,188	12s.	0d.

In all they had to pay from their two-thirds share a total of £49,584 12s. 6d. This reduction in their profits incensed Thomas Goldney in particular, since according to him, the six owners who had been appointed to look after the owners' interests in London had been profligate. Not all the owners could absent themselves from their businesses in Bristol during the Chancery Proceedings. He said "two or three of ye Managing Owners without ye privity of ye rest" had "allowed themselves large expenses and Salleries for their trouble . . ." The payment to the East India Company, with the bribe of £161 "for soliciting them to accept it" was "weakly parted with". In total the money he considered wasted amounted to £10,016 0s.[50]

Meanwhile the crews had still not received their full pay and it was nearly three years before the final stages of the accounts were completed. The crews therefore petitioned the House of Lords in June 1714 and charged the owners and officers with trying "to defraud your Petitioners of their shares . . . by vile and clandestine practices." In August 1715 the crews complained to the Lords that they had been badly treated by the Master in Chancery. They said their agent, Stephen Creagh, had threatened them with the whip, while 33 of them accused Woodes Rogers of hiding some of the treasure at Batavia. It is not immediately obvious what they thought the Lords were going to do about it.

It was perhaps inevitable that disputes would arise over the division of the spoils at the end of a long privateering voyage. The original Articles of Agreement had stated the terms of their engagement, shares being allotted according to rank or ratings. Some had been promoted since then. Some had died or run away. To some was due 'Storm Money' and 'Plunder Money', while to some unfortunates was due 'Smart Money' for wounds or disablement.[51] These complications had to be straightened out in Chancery although some attempts to do so were made outside the Courts.

Anchored in the Thames in 1711 Woodes Rogers had written in some distress to the Bristol owners on 15 October and again on 3 November inquiring how he was going to pay the men? Who owned the plunder in law now it had been seized?[52] By 6 June 1712 the chief officers had agreed on a division of plunder so that one fifth of a share would go to all who had survived till 14 April 1709 or who had died before 18 August of that year. Between that date and the 22 December following one quarter of a share would be due.[53] 'Smart Money' for the disabled and wounded was paid out from June to September 1712 to relatives, attorneys, or to the men themselves.[54]

Two years after the ships had berthed the officers and men submitted to the Master in Chancery, on 8 July 1713, their account of what shares the owners had overcharged, with the men's

'Captain Rogers's People stripping some Ladies of their Jewels in the Neighbourhood of Guiaquil' from *A new universal collection of authentic and entertaining Voyages and Travels* by Edward Cavendish Drake, 1765

objections. Above the signatures of Nathaniel Stock and John Kington they alleged that 47¼ shares had been misallocated and were owing to the officers and men.[55] The Master, in marginal notes to these claims, was clearly guided by the original Articles but seems to have allowed their case in regard to 5½ shares. In their petition to the Lords the men considered they had been badly treated by the Master in Chancery. On the other hand the two most important of the 26 Washington MSS in the Library of Congress, relating to the case, represent appeals by the owners against the findings of the Master on his General Report. In every case the Master disallowed the claim of the owners, although the sums involved were trifling and the issues might be considered petty. For example MSS 20 concerns 'Storm Money' for the taking of Guayaquil in April 1709. The owners claimed no agreement to pay a bounty was in the original Articles with the crews, and that the town was "abandoned by the Enemy upon the approach of the said Company" and not "stormed". The Master noted that two of the owners, Captains Dover and Courtney, were parties to the Council on board ship which agreed to pay 'Storm Money' and he therefore judged against the owners' claim.

It had been a significant achievement to have circumnavigated the world and brought back a Spanish treasure ship. The owners had doubled their original stake money though their agents on board, Carlton Vanbrugh and William Bath, had both died at sea. Some of the crews had been killed in action such as Woodes Rogers' brother. Some had died from sickness or from wounds, while some returned badly injured such as the young midshipman John Taylor or the landsman William Mallony.[56] Capt. Thomas Dover settled in London as a famous physician and bragged in the Jerusalem Coffee House of his exploits in the South Seas. He died in 1742 at Stanway House, Glos. Capt. Dampier was at last brought to Court by the Cresswells in 1712. Capt. Woodes Rogers sailed for the Bahamas on 11 April 1718 and was appointed Royal Governor. He died at Nassau in 1732, aged about 53. John Romsey's financial embarrassments were removed by the profits from the *Duke* and *Dutchess* and it was he who presented Bristol Cathedral with the magnificent silver candlesticks which cost £114. He retained his office as Town Clerk until his death in 1721. Thomas Goldney rebuilt Goldney House 1723–4 and died there on June 1731 aged 68.

What remains to remind us of this famous voyage? There are the two Romsey silver candlesticks on the altar in the Eastern Lady

Chapel of the Cathedral. They have the hallmark 1712 and were made by Gabriel Sleath in England and were not part of the Spanish treasure. There are the two books written in 1712 by Captains Woodes Rogers and Cooke which were based on their Journals. The real monuments to this remarkable voyage are the papers, letters and documents, ledgers, account books and wills, committee books and books of sale, sales catalogues and lists of medicines taken off prizes, which have survived in the Public Record Office at Chancery Lane. These records are a treasure in themselves and provide historians with insights into Bristol's maritime history which can hardly be bettered.

REFERENCES

Abbreviations:

Rogers' *Voyage*	Rogers, Captain Woodes, *A Cruising Voyage round the World, first to the South Seas, thence to the East Indies, and homeward by the Cape of Good Hope. Begun in 1708 and finish'd in 1711*, London, 1712.
Cooke, *Voyage*	Cooke, Captain Edward, *Voyage to the South Sea, and round the World*, 2 Vols. London, 1712.
P.R.O.	Public Record Office, Chancery Lane.
I.O.L.R.	Oriental and India Office Library and Records.
L.O.C.	Library of Congress, Washington, D.C.

1. P.R.O. C 104/36/Part 2, Orders and Instructions to Capt. Woodes Rogers.
2. P.R.O. C 104/36/Part 2, Articles of Agreement, 10 May 1708.
3. P.R.O. C 104/37/Part 1, pp. 40–43, General Accounts between the severall Owners for the *Duke* and *Dutchess* covering the Gross Sums which are to stand as a charge.
4. P.R.O. C 104/36/Part 2, Articles of Agreement, 10 May 1708.
5. P.R.O. C 104/36/Part 1, Loose letter dated 21 Feb. 1707.
6. P.R.O. C 24/1321 Part 1, Cresswell v Dampier. Deposition of Andrew Selkirk, para.17.
7. P.R.O. C 104/36/Part 2, John Parker's *Committee Book*, p. 137, Aug. 14, 1711. John Parker was a midshipman on board the *Duke*.
8. Cooke, *Voyage*, Introduction, unpaginated.
9. P.R.O. C 24/1321 Part 1, Cresswell v Dampier, 0776, Deposition of Selkirk, para. 6, 18 July 1712.
10. ibid. para. 5.
11. Rogers' *Voyage*, Introduction.
12. See P.R.O. C 104/37/Part 2, a large vellum covered book, 34cm × 24cm × 4cm with IHS on the cover referred to in Creagh v Rogers as 'B'. This contains Committee Minutes of all Councils, and each

man's entry re: shoes, tobacco, knives, stockings, snuff, combs, pipes, shirts, rugs and pillows.
13. Rogers' *Voyage* p. 4.
14. Rogers' *Voyage* p. 6.
15. Rogers' *Voyage* p. 8.
16. Rogers' *Voyage* p. 14.
17. Rogers' *Voyage* p. 25.
18. Rogers' *Voyage* p. 108.
19. P.R.O. C 24/1321 Part 1. Cresswell v Dampier, No. 0776. See C.D. Lee 'Alexander Selkirk and the last voyage of the *Cinque Ports*, galley' in *Mariner's Mirror*, Vol. 73, No. 4, No. 1987, pp. 385–399.
20. Rogers' *Voyage* p. 125.
21. P.R.O. C 104/36/Part 2, Captain Courtney's *Committee Book* June 1710.
22. ibid. Courtney's *Committee Book* 8 August 1707.
23. Rogers' *Voyage* p. 179.
24. Rogers' *Voyage* p. 28–29.
25. Rogers' *Voyage* p. 30–31, Cttee on board *Dutchess*, 8 Oct. 1708.
26. Rogers' *Voyage* p. 424.
27. ibid.
28. Rogers' *Voyage* p. 425
29. Rogers' *Voyage* p. 426. See also C 104/37 Part 1, Ref. XP 0783 CL "getting clear *most* of the men when Impress'd at Wapping".
30. Cooke *Voyage* Introduction to his patron, Robert Harley Earl of Oxford.
31. P.R.O. C 104/37/Part 2 Capt. Courtney's *Committee Book*, 20 Feb 1710/11 Cape of Good Hope.
32. ibid. Capt. Courtney's *Committee Book*.
33. Cooke *Voyage*, Vol. 1. p. 337.
34. Cooke *Voyage*, Vol. 1. p. 340.
35. P.R.O. C 104/36/Part 2, John Parker's *Committee Book*, p. 132.
36. I.O.L.R. B/51, No. 44, *East India Co. Court Minutes*, (18 April 1710–4 Apr. 1712) 25 July 1711, p. 500.
37. I.O.L.R. B/51, No. 44, *E.I.Co.Minutes*, p. 504, 1 August 1711.
38. I.O.L.R. B/51, No. 44, *E.I.Co.Minutes*, p. 502, 27 July 1711.
39. I.O.L.R. B/51, No. 44, *E.I.Co.Minutes*, p. 545, 12 Sept. 1711.
40. I.O.L.R. B/51, No. 44, *E.I.Co.Minutes*, pp. 599–600, 10 Oct 1711.
41. I.O.L.R. B/51, No. 44, *E.I.Co.Minutes*, p. 606, 17 Oct. 1711.
42. I.O.L.R. B/51, No. 44, *E.I.Co.Minutes*, p. 620, 7 Nov. 1711.
43. I.O.L.R. B/51, No. 44, *E.I.Co.Minutes*, pp. 661, 669 and 678 5 Dec., 6 Dec., and 12 Dec. 1711.
44. I.O.L.R. B/51, No. 44, *E.I.Co.Minutes*, p. 765, 26 March 1712.
45. P.R.O. C 104/37 Part 1. Ref. XP 0783 CL Stephen Creagh's Disbursements, Oct. 1711.
46. P.R.O. C 104/37 Part 2 Lib. 'A', *Account Book*, p. 44.
47. P.R.O. C 104/36 Part 1 Lib. 'F', *Book of Sales*.

48. P.R.O. C 104/37 Part 2 Lib. 'A', *Account Book*, p. 47.
49. See Rogers, Lt. Col. B.M.H. *Mariner's Mirror*, vol. 19, No. 2, 1933, p. 204.
50. P.R.O. C 104/37 Part 2, 0774, Lib.'A' The vellum bound book of Accounts with 113 pages, p. 69.
51. P.R.O. C 104/160 Smart Money for wounds and disablement.
52. P.R.O. C 104/160 Bundle 6.
53. P.R.O. C 104/160 6 June 1712. Division of Shares.
54. P.R.O. C 104/160 28 June 1712–17 Sept. 1712.
55. P.R.O. C 104/160 8 July 1713, Shares overcharged and men's Objections.
56. P.R.O. C 104/160 Woodes Rogers to J. Romsey, 27 Nov. 1711.

SOURCES

The sources for Woodes Rogers' voyage of 1708–11 are remarkably comprehensive. Chancery Masters' Exhibits were normally returned to the plaintiffs, but in the case of Creagh v Rogers the issue was essentially the distribution of the prize money after the privateering voyage. There were 209 plaintiffs being represented by Stephen Creagh, and in any case, the exhibits did not belong to them. The Lord Chancellor called in all relevant Logs, Documents, Account Books, Orders, Agreements, Council Minutes of all meetings on board, Accounts of all goods exchanged and purchased at each port of call, and a complete list of all treasure captured from the 20 prizes. Woodes Rogers and Edward Cooke retained their Journals but all the rest of the material found its way into the Public Records Office. These records are under C 104/36 (2 boxes), 37 (2 boxes), 38 and 39 which are not generally available because of their deteriorating condition, 40, and C 104/160–161.

C 104/36 Part 1 contains various letters from 1707–1708, and the *Book of Sales*, No. 'F', 37.5cm × 24cm × 10mm. It is a vellum-covered hard-backed volume of 173 pages. Part 1 also contains *The Account Current* 37cm × 24cm × 5mm. This is a soft-backed volume listing sundry merchandise imported, their Prizes and purchase goods sold. This box also contains the *List of Sales* starting 27 Feb 1711 at the Marine Coffee House, Cornhill, and the Distribution of the Prize Money of the *Duke* and *Dutchess*.

C 104/36 Part 2 contains *John Parker's Committee Book*, a vellum-bound volume, beautifully written and very easy to read. There are 137 pages and it measures 32cm × 20cm × 8mm. Part 2 contains several large parchment sheets 84cm × 71cm which are the *Articles of Agreement* between the Owners and the mariners, the landsmen and the officers of both the *Duke* and the *Dutchess*. There is the *Book of the Ships' Company* containing their respective shares and 'storm money' (15 pages), also Stephen Creagh's hearings and Court Orders (68 pages). Part 2 contains Thomas Goldney's Account with the other Owners and Proprietors and presented to the Master in Chancery. Also the box contains the *Sailing Orders* to Capt. Woodes Rogers, and the *Account Book* of the *Duke*'s Prime Costs and Outsetts. This is a soft-backed book of 34 pages, 33cm × 21cm × 5mm. The so-called *Book of Objections* 32cm × 20cm × 5mm is soft-backed, and has only 5 used pages!

C 104/37/Part 1 contains the *Account Book* for the *Dutchess*, showing monies paid to the crew, monies due to Stephen Creagh, monies due for 'Plunder Money'. It is soft-backed and measures 37cm × 24.5cm × 5mm. The box contains the *General Accounts* for the *Duke* and *Dutchess* 1708–20 June 1717. It is a large book of 53 pages, covered in vellum, and measuring 37.5cm × 24.5cm × 2cm, and includes the prime costs of building the two boats. There is the *Account Book* for payments in Holland, for 'Smart Money', and for moneys paid to the Custom House. It measures 38cm × 25cm × 5 mm. There is also the *Accounts of Prizes and Prize Goods*, called Book 3, vellum covered, which itemises the sales, and is in very good condition. It measures 38cm × 25cm × 2.5cm.

C 104/37/Part 2 holds a large book, vellum bound, of 113 pages, referred to as 'Lib.A'. It measures 41.5cm × 27.5cm × 2cm. The book is an *Account of goods bought by the Duke and Dutchess* at each stopping place round the world. It contains a list of medical stores taken off the *Ascension*, and lists of 'storm money' and 'plunder money'. The box contains a *Deed* appointing John Ward and James Campbell, and Stephen Creagh, to act for various parties. This is a parchment sheet. There are two soft-backed books containing *Accounts* of all men's wages, shares etc and measuring 38cm × 25cm × 5mm.

37/Part 2 also contains the *Institution of a Council* "for directing the affaires of the Ships *Duke* and *Dutchess*, Friggetts, in this present Voyage to America". There are also the *Ships' Rolls* for the *Duke* and *Dutchess*, listing the men's pay.

C 104/37/Part 2 holds the *Committee Minutes of all Councils held at sea, 1708–11*. This large vellum covered book, referred to in Court as No. 'B', is 34cm × 24cm × 4cm. On the front are the letters I.H.S., and inside the cover is the name John Miller. The book contains, in addition to the Minutes, copies of all the letters sent and received, and each man's entries re. tobacco, shoes, knives, stockings, combs, pipes, shirts, rugs, pillows, and snuff. It contains a manifest of all that was on board the *Marquis*. Since some of the pages are bleached this may be the Journal referred to by Woodes Rogers as being kept open on view to all officers and crew.

C 104/160–161, Chancery Masters' Exhibits, *Creagh v Rogers*, consist of three boxes, 160 and 161 Parts 1 and 2.

Box 160 contains letters, papers and documents including: Captain Woodes Rogers' description of the voyage up to 28 July 1709, written to

Alderman John Batchelor: *A List of the Negroes*, names, sex, and condition, taken off the *Ascension*, 28 July 1709; Capt. Courtney's and Capt. Cooke's descriptions of the voyage up to the arrival at the Cape of Good Hope, 8 Feb. 1711; the *Account of what shares the Owners overcharged*, with the Officers' and Men's objections, 8 July 1713; *Lists of 'Smart Money'* paid to the wounded, 5 June 1712 and money paid to relatives of those who had died on the voyage, 6 June 1712; *Medicines taken out of prizes* for use in the *Duke*, *Dutchess* and *Marquis*, 22 July 1709; *Instructions* from the owners to James Hollidge, Philipp Freke and John Duckinfield in Holland, 16 Aug. 1711; The legal case for the *Duke* and *Dutchess*, addressed to their Counsel; *Letters from Woodes Rogers* at anchor in the Thames, to the Bristol owners, 15 Oct., 3 Nov. 1711; *All letters addressed home from Carlton Vanbrugh*, the owners' agent on board (1 bundle); Copies of all Woodes Rogers' letters written while at sea (2 bundles); *Copies of all letters written during the Court proceedings* from London to Bristol by James Hollidge, John Romsey, Thomas Palmer, and Edward Acton.

The two sections of Box 161 contain a number of vellum covered volumes, 'C', 'D', and 'E' listing the *contents of the treasure chests*, and the contents of each of the prizes captured; the *Sales Catalogues* of all the goods to be viewed in the several warehouses to be sold 'by the Candle' at the Marine Coffee House, Burchin Lane, Wed. 27 Feb. 1711 to Mon. 20 Oct. 1712; the initial stores of the *Duke*, *Dutchess* and *Marquis*; the *Wills* of various seamen, including those of two Spanish prisoners, witnessed by Woodes Rogers; *Capt. Courtney's Accounts* of disbursements on the voyage at Batavia, the South Seas, and in Holland.

C 24/1321 Part 1 Cresswell v Dampier. This box contains the *Depositions* of Alexander Selkirk, William Sheltram, John Welbe, Ralph Clift, William Funnell and many others, in the case against Dampier.

Oriental and India Office Library and Record, 197 Blackfriars Rd., S.E.1 8NG. The India Office holds the *Court Book Minutes of the Governors of the East India Company*, under B/51. The volumes are vellum bound and very large, 46cm × 30cm × 9cm. Number 44 contains the minutes for April 1710 to April 1712, pp. 500–765. The volumes are beautifully written and very clear. They are also on Microfilm 9233.

House of Lords Library holds the *Petitions* by the crews of the *Duke* and *Dutchess*, 17 June, 1714 and 31 August 1715.

Library of Congress, Washington, D.C. There are 26 documents connected with the finances of the voyage of the *Duke* and *Dutchess*. Three list payments to officers and crew while at Batavia, some list the small claims for work done while unloading and warehousing. The most important are the appeals by the owners against the findings of the Master on his General Report.

Goldney Papers. These are held at four centres. Papers relating to Bristol estates can be seen at Bristol Record Office under BRO 38640. Papers such as Goldney III's Day Book can be seen at the Wiltshire Record Office, By-the-Sea Rd., Trowbridge, together with all papers relating to the Chippenham estate. Goldney House holds a number of papers as does the University of Bristol Library Archives. I have corresponded with the last surviving Goldney with regard to the letter relating to the *Duke* and *Dutchess* shown to Lt. Col. B.M.H. Rogers in 1932 by Sir Frederick Goldney, and reported by him in the *Mariner's Mirror*, Vol. 19, No. 2, 1933, but we have failed to find it.

Woodes Rogers' *A Cruising Voyage* . . . London, 1712. There is a copy of the 1712 edition in Bristol Reference Library, Braikenridge collection 10651, Stock Room 21, Accession Number 4400.

Edward Cooke's *Voyage to the South Sea* . . . 2 Vols 1712. There is a copy of the 1712 edition in Bristol Reference Library, Braikenridge Collection, Stock Room 138, Accession Number 10649–50.

British Musuem. Sloane 3236 (Capt. William Dampier's Journal).

Archivo de Indias, Seville. These have been researched by Bryan Little, (See his *Crusoe's Captain, Being the Life of Woodes Rogers, Seaman, Trader, Colonial Governor*. 1960.) Arch. de Ind. Seville, Section V are papers transferred to Seville from Simancas from 1785 onwards; VI and VIa are papers from the Escribania de Camara of the Consejo de Indias. The papers relate to Rogers' attack on Guayaquil etc., in various bundles (legajos) dealing with viceregal correspondence, the residencia on the viceroyalty of the Marques de Castelldosrius and the case against the corregidor D.Ieronimo Bosa y Solis.

Museo Naval, Madrid. This was also researched by Bryan Little, op. cit., for MS.Misc. 194 Item 8. This is a transcript of the narrative of two hostages taken at Guayaquil and released early in 1710.